# Has service user participation made a difference to social care services?

*Sarah Carr*

First published in Great Britain in March 2004 by the Social Care Institute for Excellence (SCIE)

Social Care Institute for Excellence
1st Floor
Goldings House
2 Hay's Lane
London SE1 2HB
UK
www.scie.org.uk

© Social Care Institute for Excellence 2004

British Library Cataloguing in Publication Data

A catalogue record for this book is available from the British Library

ISBN 1 904812 10 4

**Sarah Carr** is a Research Analyst at SCIE.

The right of Sarah Carr to be identified as author of this work has been asserted by her in accordance with the 1988 Copyright, Designs and Patents Act.

All rights reserved. No part of this publication may be reproduced or transmitted in any form or by any means, electronic, mechanical, photocopying, recording or otherwise, or stored in any retrieval system of any nature, without prior permission of the publisher.

Produced by The Policy Press
University of Bristol
Fourth Floor, Beacon House
Queen's Road
Bristol BS8 1QU
UK
www.policypress.org.uk

Printed and bound in Great Britain by Hobbs the Printers Ltd, Southampton.

# Contents

Acknowledgements — iv

Executive summary: key themes and findings — v

1. Introduction — 1

2. Methods — 3
   2.1. Reference key for reviews — 3
   2.2. Note on format — 4

3. Background — 5
   3.1. Policy context — 5
   3.2. Participation concepts — 5
   3.3. The social model of disability and service user priorities — 5

4. Main findings — 7
   4.1. Extent of current knowledge — 7
   4.2. Intrinsic benefits of participation — 8
   4.3. Feedback — 9
   4.4. Participation and change at an individual level — 10
      4.4.1. Choice and control — 10
      4.4.2. Direct Payments — 11
      4.4.3. Complaints — 12
   4.5. Organisational commitment and responsiveness — 13
   4.6. Power relations — 14
   4.7. Partnership or consultancy? — 17
   4.8. Conflict and expectations — 19
   4.9. Diversity and marginalisation — 21

5. The Wiltshire and Swindon User Network: an example in practice — 25

6. Conclusion: messages for policy and practice — 27
   6.1. Messages from the research for policy makers — 28

Additional references — 29

Appendix — 31

# Acknowledgements

We would like to thank all those who contributed to the production of this report, for their comments, advice and insight. Particular thanks go to Clare Evans who advised on the final overview and to Carlisle People First, Greater London Action on Disability, Older People Researching Social Issues, Voice for the Child in Care, Age Concern, the Tizard Centre and Hertfordshire County Council.

We are also grateful to Dr Stuart Anderson, Dr Mike Crawford and Angela Sweeney for their assistance in obtaining the NHS Service Delivery and Organisation Research and Development Programme (NHS SDO) review work.

# Executive summary: key themes and findings

This summary brings together the key themes and findings from the synthesis of six literature reviews on the impact of user participation on change and improvement in social care services. Reviews on older people, children and young people, people with learning difficulties and disabled people were commissioned by the Social Care Institute for Excellence (SCIE). Reviews on mental health service user participation and on general user/consumer involvement were commissioned by NHS Service Delivery and Organisation Research and Development Programme (NHS SDO).

The conclusion at the end of this Position paper (see pp 27-8) suggests some ways forward. In addition, the findings from this Position paper will form the basis for Practice guides on service user participation, which will provide examples of how to build on current progress.

## Messages for policy and practice

Efforts to involve people in the planning and development of the services they use are taking place across the UK. However, the impact of that participation on the change and improvement of social care services is yet to be properly monitored and evaluated. Much progress has been made in establishing the principle of service user participation and developing ways of doing this. There is now a second stage that will entail looking at how organisations, systems and practice need to change in order to respond to participation.

At local and regional levels policy makers would be advised to integrate change mapping and feedback into the whole participation process. Monitoring and evaluation techniques should be developed with service users.

Messages from research show *the need for a range of models of involvement, depending on the level of activity that participants wish to commit. What is important is that the choice is there, and that the involvement – or partnership – is real* (R2) (see pp 2-4 for an explanation of the reference sources). User participation should relate clearly to a decision that the organisation plans to make, and is open to influence. It should be made clear what service users may or may not be able to change.

Professionals are now interacting with service users as partners in strategic planning arenas as well as at front-line service delivery level. It appears that involving front-line staff in participation strategies and providing user-led awareness training could help improve relations at both strategic and service delivery level. The role of professional allies could be usefully explored.

Challenges to traditional professional modes of thinking and operating are emerging as a result of participation. Organisational cultures and structures need to respond and change in order to accommodate new partnerships and new ways of working with people who have often been oppressed and marginalised. The service user movement seems to be exposing the limitations of traditional, fragmented service categories for organising participation designed to promote strategic change. Participation provides a unique opportunity for organisations to develop through user-led critical enquiry using the social model of disability, ideas about control, oppression, rights, poverty and citizenship.

## Extent of current knowledge

There is a general lack of research and evaluation on the impact and outcomes of service user participation. Little seems to be formally recorded at local, regional or national levels and the influence of user participation on transforming services has not been the subject of any major UK research studies to date.

There is some knowledge about participation techniques but little or no examination of the relationship between the process and the achievement of tangible user-led change. This is not to say that certain participation initiatives are not contributing to the improvement of services for the people who use them, but that those changes are not being monitored.

## Intrinsic benefits of participation

Where monitoring is taking place, it is often related to participation processes rather than outcomes. Some agencies may only be focusing on the intermediate aspects of how individuals experience the process, rather than combining this evaluation with that of impact and outcome. While intrinsic benefits are important, the true effectiveness of these processes to promote change and impact on improvement remains largely untested.

## Feedback

Service users say they need to receive feedback as an integral part of the participation process, but this does not appear to be happening. Agencies should see monitoring of impact and meaningful feedback as a vital constituent of process, as it related to engagement and commitment. When little or nothing is communicated back to participants, this can have a negative effect on their motivation, trust and confidence.

## Participation and change at an individual level

The groundswell for change can originate at individual service level. Exercise of choice as an individual 'welfare consumer' remains restricted, particularly if you are from a black or minority ethnic group or are lesbian or gay. The ability to make choices can be limited by a lack of information about options and a lack of support for decision making. Professionally led assessment of eligibility for services can pose difficulties for exercising choice and control.

The implementation of Direct Payments by local authorities and the extent to which they are publicised is inconsistent. Good support systems, including access to advisers and peer support networks, are needed. The limited choice and support has, in some cases, led to the establishment of user-controlled service providers and services by and for black and minority ethnic people.

Local authorities have formal complaints procedures intended to enable individuals to exercise some control over the quality of services. However, such procedures may not be functioning to the advantage of the service user or the agency. Research suggests that complaints procedures can remain unknown, inaccessible or intimidating to service users.

## Organisational commitment and responsiveness

Despite the overall lack of research or recorded knowledge illuminating the relationship between user participation and service change and improvement, the reviews show strong indications of why change may not be occurring. A lack of organisational responsiveness is an issue common to all the reviews. A fundamental political commitment to change should be driving participation initiatives.

## Power relations

Power issues underlie the majority of identified difficulties with effective user-led change. User participation initiatives require continual awareness of the context of power relations in which they are being conducted. Exclusionary structures, institutional practices and professional attitudes can still affect the extent to which service users can influence change. It appears that power sharing can be difficult within established mainstream structures, formal consultation mechanisms and traditional ideologies.

The relative values placed on different types of expertise and language and the professional assumptions about decision-making competence can make it difficult for users to be heard, or to make an impact on decisions. Managerial concern about achieving 'representativeness' (although not necessarily diversity in terms of culture, race, sexuality or disability) can also impede the progress of user-led change.

## Partnership or consultancy?

In some cases there is a risk of user participation initiatives being conducted as externalised consultation exercises to approve of professional service planning and policy proposals, rather than enabling service users to be integral partners for their formulation.

Embedded, continuous but varied participation approaches which engage service users as partners in decision making seem to have most potential for influencing change. Service users want to choose how they are represented. Agencies are recommended to re-examine their notion of service users who are thought to be 'hard to reach'. Some service users may lack structures of representation or the knowledge and support to empower them to participate.

## Conflict and expectations

Dissatisfaction and even conflict may be an inevitable part of the user participation process. Service users and professionals can have conflicting priorities. Limited funds and service remits can restrain the degree to which service users may be able to influence changes in services. Organisations should be clear from the outset about what can and cannot be done as a result of participation and the true extent of user influence in the given circumstances. Similarly, service users should be empowered to voice their limits and expectations.

Development of mutual understanding and trust takes time. Working to timetables determined without service users may result in the exclusion of some people or limit their effective participation. Organisations and their managers should support front-line practitioners to focus on user concerns. It is important for agencies to support and fund user groups to maintain their independence and critical function.

## Diversity and marginalisation

Attention to the diversity of service users in terms of race, culture and sexuality is lacking both in mainstream services and participation initiatives. This relates to both diversity within user groups and the relative lack of knowledge about user participation for marginalised people. There are also difficulties for black and minority ethnic people and lesbian and gay people with disabilities, who are also working on the margins of a predominantly white, culturally heterosexual user movement. The challenge to mainstream services is to creatively engage all marginalised peoples, the concerns of whom often extend beyond service provision to creating positive social and political identities in the face of discrimination.

# Introduction

The positive contribution service users can make to social care planning and development is now recognised in government policy. Service users are taking an active role in efforts to improve both health and social care services. However, the level and extent of effective service user participation in changing and improving services is inconsistent. This can be both change and improvement in immediate services and in the culture and attitudes of the agencies and staff who deliver those services. User participation in research, training and education are also important for service change and improvement: these topics are not covered within the scope of this overview but will be the subject of other work. Similarly, the experiences of carers, parents and supporters will be the subject of later Knowledge reviews.

The remit of the Social Care Institute for Excellence (SCIE) is to develop a knowledge base for social care, so that evidence on what works best is available to everyone involved. There are many guides on how to involve service users in developing social care services, but less is known about the outcomes of that involvement. This report examines the evidence about the impact service user participation may have had on creating better quality social care services. Part of this includes looking at why change may or may not have happened.

This report is a SCIE Position paper. SCIE Position papers give an analysis, drawing on available knowledge, of a particular policy question. This particular Position paper draws together four Knowledge reviews commissioned by SCIE. A SCIE Knowledge review takes a systematic approach to the analysis of knowledge on a particular topic.

The reviews describe the material available (the evidence) and the findings drawn from the evidence. The evidence can be from a range of sources including research literature, practice, and the knowledge held by users. These SCIE Knowledge reviews cover older people, children and young people, people with learning difficulties and disabled people. This Position paper also incorporates findings from two NHS Service Delivery and Organisation Research and Development Programme (NHS SDO) literature reviews concerning mental health service users and user and consumer involvement in managing change generally.

The aim of this work is to give an overview or synthesis of these reviews in order to provide a comprehensive, accessible account of what is currently known about the impact of service user participation on change and improvement in social care services. It will also provide a basis for SCIE Practice guides on service user participation.

# Methods

At the beginning of this project a scoping exercise took place to see if any similar work was taking place and the reviews being commissioned by the NHS SDO were identified. SCIE did not want to duplicate this work so decided to commission work to complement these existing reviews. As a result SCIE commissioned reviews entitled 'user involvement in promoting change and enhancing the quality of services' for older people, children and young people, people with learning difficulties and disabled people.

When SCIE commissioned the reviews authors were asked to look at different types of literature. It was felt to be very important to ensure that accounts from service users that may not be published in the conventional way were included. Therefore the Knowledge reviews cover a wide range of relevant materials, including:

- research studies of the processes and outcomes of methods of user involvement;
- descriptive/analytical accounts of activities and developments;
- knowledge produced by user groups;
- best practice; and
- accounts that may not be published or officially written up.

The reviews drew on materials concerning user involvement in England and Wales along with relevant literature focusing on Northern Ireland and Scotland. The date range for literature and accounts was from 1992 to 2002, with seminal work before those dates included where appropriate. The majority of material covered statutory and voluntary social care services, with limited coverage of the independent sector.

There was service user participation at all stages of production. A service user had equal decision-making power on the tender board that chose the successful proposals. SCIE required service users to have significant involvement in the commissioned work, and included this in the decision criteria for the tender board. In some cases service users authored the reviews. The drafts were independently assessed by people with experience as service users in the particular area under review (for example, the report on older people was assessed by older people). This overview report was authored by someone with experience of using services and was independently assessed by a service user. Everyone SCIE invited to take part in the selection and review process was paid fairly and equally, and all expenses met where needed.

## 2.1. Reference key for reviews

This overview report includes direct quotations from the (unpublished) reviews. The codes used in the text correspond with the following titles:

R1 = Danso, C., Greaves, H., Howell, S., Ryan, M., Sinclair, R. and Tunnard, J. (2003) *The involvement of children and young people in promoting change and enhancing the quality of services: A research report for SCIE from the National Children's Bureau*.

R2 = Janzon, K. and Law, S. (2003) *Older people influencing social care: Aspirations and realities. Research review on user involvement in promoting change and enhancing the quality of social care services, Final report for SCIE.*

R3 = Williams, V. (2003) *Has anything changed? User involvement in promoting change and enhancing the quality of services for people with learning difficulties, Final report for SCIE.*

R4 = Barnes, C., Mercer, G. and Din, I. (2003) *Research review on user involvement in promoting change and enhancing the quality of social care services for disabled people, Final report for SCIE.*

R5 = Rose, D., Fleischmann, P., Tonkiss, F., Campbell, P. and Wykes, T. (2003) *Review of the literature: User and carer involvement in change management in a mental health context: Report to NHS Service Delivery and Organisation Research and Development Programme* (NHS SDO).

R6 = Crawford, M., Rutter, D. and Thelwall, S. (2003) *User involvement in change management: A review of the literature, Report to NHS Service Delivery and Organisation Research and Development Programme* (NHS SDO).

Please see the Appendix for further details.

## 2.2. Note on format

The text of this report contains both bold and italic characters. The passages in italic are direct quotations from the original reviews, referenced using the codes explained above. Bold is used to highlight key points within the text, which may include the sentences in italics.

# Background

## 3.1. Policy context

Over the past 20 years several major pieces of legislation have made service user participation a requirement in many aspects of the UK health and social services. The first of these was the 1990 National Health Service and Community Care Act, which made consultation with service users a legislative duty for local authorities. Later, increased requirements for active service user (and carer) participation in service development and regulation were set out in government directives on Best Value for local authorities, and the legislation associated with the New Labour public service 'modernisation' agenda.

## 3.2. Participation concepts

There are long-standing debates about the distinctions to be drawn between the different types and levels of user participation. It ranges on a continuum from consultation on an individual level including feedback about services, surveys and complaints through participation in the planning and development of services to user control and management of services[1]. Distinctions have been identified between 'consumerist' and 'democratic' approaches and agency-led and user-led initiatives, both having implications for power and control. Democratic initiatives involve service users influencing and making decisions at strategic levels, while consumerist approaches focus more narrowly on consulting people about the services they receive. **Gradually there has been a move away from the idea of just consulting people about agency-led proposals to the notion of developing services in active partnership with those who use them;** however, this is not always translated into practice.

Messages from research show *the need for a range of models of involvement, depending on the level of activity that participants wish to commit. What is important is that the choice is there, and that the involvement – or partnership – is real* (R2). Further to this it has been emphasised that *participation needs to be appropriate to its context and to take account of the issues involved, the objectives sought and the people who make up the target group. Different kinds of participation might be appropriate for different parts of a project or at different stages in its development* (R1).

## 3.3. The social model of disability and service user priorities

The social model of disability was originally conceived by the disability movement as a tool for gaining insight into their situation and to recognise how they were oppressed: *It is society which disables physically impaired people. Disability is something imposed on top of our impairments*[2]. **The idea that it is society that erects barriers and restricts the options and activities of disabled people has been used by others who are disempowered by social, cultural and physical structures to interpret their situations.** For example, *society often disables older people simply because they are old and by assuming they cannot perform certain tasks and activities* (R2), and the user movement of mental health service users *tries to reframe a negative social identity as positive and strong* (R5). **The social model of disability has**

**therefore become fundamental for the service user movement and the demand for independent living and citizenship rights.** When service users understand participation as active citizenship it *goes beyond their rights as users of social services to assert their broader rights as citizens and as people*[3]. *Service users may [then] have a dual identity as consumers of services, and as citizens to whom such services are accountable* (R5). The social model of disability has implications for the way in which services have been organised and participation initiatives conceived: as one review points out *[community care] planning bodies were based upon 'traditional' service divisions, emphasising the separate incapacities of client groups rather than the common experience of social restrictions* (R6).

**There are clear preferences among people who use social care services for support and assistance to live independently, rather than 'care', which implies dependency.** For some people, particularly older people, families and mental health service users, 'preventative' support work rather than 'crisis' intervention is seen as crucial. The service user movement has been clear about promoting *the right of disadvantaged people to support and equal access to the ordinary things of life*[4]. This is consistent with the social model of disability as described above. Literature from the service user movement and elsewhere provides a general consensus that positive change needs to be felt at the point of service delivery if it is to be meaningful: *Service users are ... interested in what services can help them achieve, in the purposes and outcomes of such services, in the effect on their lives*[5]. This is reflected in what the reviews found out about the approach of service users to desired outcomes. Research has shown that *older people want to help to support their independence, rather than care, and want services to be more responsive to individual preferences and changing circumstances* (R2), and that for people with learning difficulties *their goals for a home, friendships, work and choices are not extraordinary, measured by the quality of life we would all expect* (R3). The review for people with learning difficulties also warns those who are organising participation to promote change in policy and practice that *policy may often outstrip what is happening for people at grassroots level, and it is important to look behind the glamour of board meetings and conferences, into the reality of people's lived experiences* (R3). Similarly, for children and young people *attention should be paid to the issues that children see as important, often different to the issues about which adults are most concerned. For children, day-to-day matters and issues of contact with families are of key importance* (R1).

# Main findings

## 4.1. Extent of current knowledge

All reviews conclude that **there is a lack of research, monitoring and evaluation on the impact and outcomes of service user participation in general.** Very little seems to be formally recorded at local, regional or national levels and the direct influence of user participation on transforming services has not been the subject of any major UK research studies to date. For example, the 2000 Children Act says that *there are as yet no routine statistical collections that inform the Quality Protects objective about participation* (R1).

**There is some knowledge about participation techniques but little or no examination of the relationship between the process and the achievement of tangible user-led change. This is not to say that certain participation initiatives are not contributing to the improvement of services for the people who use them, but that those changes are not being properly monitored and evaluated.** Monitoring impact and auditing change as a result of service user participation does not appear to be recognised as a constituent part of the *whole* participation process. As the following findings from the reviews show there is a general consensus about this situation.

Of the participation of children and young people, *reports tend to convey optimism about the values of … changes, and an assumption that there are positive outputs from participatory activity…. But the lack of evaluation leaves the causal link unproven. And there is very little written about improvements in the quality of service received* (R1). Additionally, *there is consensus among reviewers that the emphasis is on process rather than outcomes, either desired or achieved, and that those that do measure outcomes rely on perceptions of those involved rather than objective measures identified at the start of the exercise…*(R1). The literature for people with learning difficulties suggests that *there seems to be a general consensus that to date it has been impossible to assess the impact of inclusive approaches to research or to planning, largely because outcomes are not always documented, or may be recorded in non-conventional ways* (R3). Within this small body of literature, *knowledge of outcomes is by far the most significant gap. The reports of specific changes are haphazard and incomplete. There is currently far more documentation relating to the process than to the achievement of gains in the lives of people with learning difficulties. This may be a necessary stage and it is important to get the processes right. However, it is equally important to ensure that participation forums such as partnership boards move on to substance, and that we build up more knowledge of change* (R3). There is an identical situation with older people's involvement where *the broad consensus emerging from researchers, inspectors and service users is that there is little evidence overall that involvement of older people is transforming services to reflect their expressed preferences and/or priorities* (R2).

For disabled people, *the literature search produced a striking absence of studies evaluating the relationship between disabled user involvement in social care services and specific quality and outcomes…. Instead of using quasi-experimental research designs, the favoured approach has been to gather survey or qualitative data on the perceived impact of user involvement. This is typically in the form of ratings by service users, managers and professional providers of their satisfaction with the process and/or outcomes* (R4). In the field of participation by people who use mental health services there is *a relatively weak evidence base for the impact of user involvement on organisational change…*(R5). The review found that *the outcomes identified in the literature are hardly ever-measurable ones, indicating the difficulty of measuring cultural and organisational change and its sustainability. The majority of papers indicated that the outcomes of user involvement in change management are unclear or unknown* (R5). Finally, the NHS SDO multi-sector literature review *found little evidence of independent research in any of the sectors … examined. Most of the reports were discussion papers that illustrated points raised with reference to brief case studies* (R6).

Overall, it appears that **where monitoring is taking place, it is related to participation processes rather than outcomes. This suggests that some agencies may only be focusing on the intermediate aspects of how individuals experience the process, rather than combining this evaluation with that of impact and outcome.** The true effectiveness of these processes to promote user-led change and impact on service improvement remains largely untested.

## 4.2. Intrinsic benefits of participation

**One difficulty identified in the majority of the reviews is the tendency for agencies to focus on the 'intrinsic benefits' of participation, that is to say, how the people have gained personally from the experience of participation, rather than on the change achieved.** The NHS SDO general literature review found that where participation outcomes were being monitored, *this was generally in the form of qualitative process evaluation of user involvement initiatives or surveys of service users and providers involved in the process* (R6). Service user participation exercises can be an opportunity for often excluded and disenfranchised people to have a say in matters of direct concern to their lives. This can be a positive experience for the individual, such as the older person who said *"that's one of the best things that's ever happened to me, is getting to go there and voice my opinion"* (R6). The reviews reveal some positive developments in this area.

Evaluation of some participation initiatives for older people have demonstrated *intrinsic benefits for the users related to social contact, opportunities for learning and developments of self-esteem* (R2). Similarly for children and young people the SCIE review found that *there is substantial evidence that children and young people perceive that they have gained in self-confidence, self-belief, knowledge and skills, education and employment. There are also accounts of improved peer relations, the development of group skills, and the erosion of gender divisions between participating young people* (R1).

For mental health service users, however, the notion of 'intrinsic benefits' is sometimes translated into user participation as 'therapy', an understanding that is thought to have negative consequences: *there is an argument to be made that some 'supportive' professional attitudes can limit the impact and effectiveness by reducing this to individual therapeutic outcomes. That is, user involvement may be endorsed by professionals as performing a therapeutic or rehabilitative function in enhancing individuals' skills, competence and self-esteem* (R5). For people with learning difficulties the practice of self-advocacy and speaking up is an important process for individuals, which can contribute positively to building confidence and esteem. However, it is also noted that the purpose of self-advocacy is to produce change and that *involvement must be about a collective voice for people with learning difficulties, not just about individuals...* (R3). Often, when self-advocates speak up and participate, it is not only for the intermediate individual benefits, but to demand service change. **The power of the collective approach of service user organisations to participation is an important consideration. Individuals can feel empowered through collective involvement** to instigate change and improvement in their own service provision.

It has been argued that *the success of user involvement projects cannot be measured solely by reference to objective changes with service agencies* (R6). However, findings emerging from the reviews suggest that while individual experiences are being monitored in some cases, objective changes to service quality remain unmeasured. The review for disabled people showed that *it is evident that much attention has been given by service providers over recent years to the process of user consultation but relatively less concern about why to consult or to what end. If the reason for consulting disabled people is not clearly thought through then the form of consultation becomes more important than the content or outcome* (R4). While attention may be paid to the quality of the process for the individual, outcomes and change as a result of participation may not be realised.

**Individual service user experience of participation mechanisms should be monitored, so that agencies can learn from both positive and negative responses and improve the process.** User research in the voluntary sector has shown that *by frequently asking themselves and others what worked well and why, users and managers developed systems of continuous feedback, which enabled them to learn, and adapt*[6]. Although intrinsic benefits to individual service users can be indicated, this is not the sole purpose of participation. The reviews positively indicate that **it is important to monitor both process and outcome, and note that the success of participation should not be reduced to individual at the expense of organisational outcomes.** Agencies are advised against satisfaction with 'intrinsic benefits' alone, but should respond to what service users have said during the participation process. As the review for children and young people emphasises, *ensuring participation is not simply an end in itself but a means to change* (R1).

## 4.3. Feedback

The reviews show that **service users require feedback about the impact of their participation.** Service users say they need not only to feel the changes in their lives as a result of improvement at individual or service level, but also need to receive feedback as an integral part of the participation process. The Audit Commission has stressed the importance of change beginning and ending with users or consumers[7]. Emerging findings show that **agencies should see monitoring of impact and meaningful feedback as a vital constituent of the user participation initiative, as it is related to engagement and commitment.** The research examined in the reviews suggests that lack of feedback can result in frustration and cynicism about the practice of service user participation as well as potential disengagement from the process altogether. **When little or nothing is communicated back to participants, this can have a negative effect on their motivation and confidence.**

The NHS SDO general literature review on user participation in managing change reports *there is general agreement that in order to achieve sustained involvement of users it is important to provide adequate time and resources to make their contribution and to ensure that those taking part receive feedback on how their contribution affected service delivery. Emphasis in the literature on process, rather than outcomes, of user involvement suggests that users often do not have the information to judge whether their participation made a difference* (R6). In the case of older people the Audit Commission has reported that although service users experience an increase in listening and consultation, they are not getting adequate feedback and are still waiting to feel associated improvements in the services they receive. In this case, frequent consultation without tangible results has led to a continued feeling of disempowerment and sometimes cynicism and disengagement[8].

This situation is common to many service users and has led to criticism from different groups of people. For example, the self-advocacy movement of people with learning difficulties has a very action-oriented approach. *Self-advocacy should be about action – ie how to achieve real and long-lasting change* (R3). When the action taken as a result of participation is not communicated, self-advocates often report dissatisfaction and frustration. For children and young people, *one of the main deterrents identified is that children assume, on the basis of experience that nothing will change: they will not be listened to – if they are – nothing will happen. There is some evidence of increased cynicism after children have been involved in consultation that is tokenistic* (R1). *Children are helped by being clear about the process of decision making, about the reason for their involvement and where their opinions will go, what will be done with them, and how and when they will receive feedback* (R1). Disabled people too report that *there is a further risk of 'involvement fatigue' with too many consultation initiatives that have little impact on service standards or profiles* (R4).

For people whose lives are often characterised by levels of disempowerment, a service user participation process that reinforces this feeling could be harmful. **The reviews emphasise the importance of recognising that participation is a two-way process and of acting accordingly.**

## 4.4. Participation and change at an individual level

At individual 'consumer' level, community care legislation has given adult service users the right to involvement in constructing their own care or support packages, the idea being to provide choice and greater flexibility to the consumer. Legislation concerning services for children and young people says that they should have the opportunity to voice their preferences. It has been suggested that by using services as individuals, people are already participating in change and development[9]. Research from the learning difficulties field has shown that *individual life changes can create a groundswell for change, and so methodologies such as person-centred planning and Direct Payments that will help individuals and families move forward are very important* (R3). Some of the SCIE commissioned reviews looked at the individual service aspects of participation in change, in the context of the wider participation agenda. This section briefly examines the report findings on how participation at the level of the individual consumer of social care services may have contributed to service change. The reports for this overview identified the following areas: choice and control; Direct Payments; and complaints.

### 4.4.1. Choice and control

So far evidence in this area is patchy but inspection reports, qualitative studies and accounts from service users suggest that **exercise of choice as an individual 'welfare consumer' remains restricted, particularly if you are from a black or minority ethnic group or are lesbian or gay.**

There still appears to be a lack of opportunity for people to have a say in their own services. As regards the exercise of choice for older people, service users report that they feel 'consulted' rather than 'involved' and *for some there was a sense of powerlessness in what to them was a complex or confusing system* (R2). Research also indicated that *users were restricting their choices at assessment because of a perception that local authorities had limited resources for community care* (R2). For black and minority ethnic older people, research shows that there is still poor communication and availability of information about available services as well as indication that minority ethnic older people are less likely to find an appropriate care provider. There is still an assumption that black and minority ethnic families 'look after their own'. Overall, for older people, *what appears at a strategic level as 'more choice', because of an increase in providers, at the service user level, is no more than a potential for choice* (R2).

The participation of children and young people in their individual care planning also has identified limitations. The report emphasises that *it is a cause for concern that a wide range of studies report that children continue to feel that they are not listened to despite a statutory framework for participation…* (R1). Although there is some evidence that children feel able to influence decisions at family group conferences, *consultation and involvement in decision making is largely organised around formal processes such as reviews. Children perceive these meetings as boring, repetitive, intrusive and also frightening* (R1). It is noted that the processes to allow children and young people to exercise choice may not be working well for those who are younger, from a minority ethnic background, disabled or looked after.

For children and young people and people with learning difficulties, **the ability to make choices was often limited by a lack of information about options and preparatory information for meetings, along with a lack of support or creative communication in decision making.** The review for people with learning difficulties notes that service users as consumers can be *pervasively marginalised by lack of knowledge about their own situation* (R3), knowledge vital for enabling choice and control. **Disabled people have found that assessment of eligibility for services can pose difficulties for exercising choice and control**: *at the individual level, the imposition of strict eligibility and assessment criteria for access to support services seriously undermines the notion of meaningful participation and choice* (R4). *Decisions about access to assessments are often influenced by service criteria based on risk and budgetary concerns* (R4). There is evidence that **there can be potential for improvement if users are involved in developing assessment and care management forms**[10]. Research also points to the importance of creatively engaging service users in the continual consultation and review of how the care or support is working for them, not just at initial assessment stage. Finally there is some indication, particularly for potential black and minority ethnic service users, that *consultation strategies may stop at needs assessment, with professionals planning how needs should be met, often within institutional frameworks* (R6).

### 4.4.2. Direct Payments

Through the collective campaigning efforts of service users (particularly disabled people and people with learning difficulties) and their allies, Direct Payments were introduced in 1996. They constitute a meaningful advance for the extent to which entitled service users can exercise control over their support and assistance in order to live independently. Disabled people, people with learning difficulties, mental health service users and now older people are entitled to use local authority funds to purchase their own personal assistance. **Although there is a general agreement among service users that Direct Payments are a very positive development, their implementation by local authorities and the extent to which they are publicised remains inconsistent.** They are also *cash limited. Once the cash ceiling is reached users are at risk of having their support withdrawn* (R4).

The review for disabled people showed that *the provision is uneven geographically with, for example, disproportionately more personal assistant users in South East England. Many local authorities have been extremely reluctant to introduce Direct Payments, while some within the disabled community have found it difficult to access payment schemes. These include older disabled people, those from minority ethnic groups and lesbians and gay men with disabilities. There are recurring obstacles that include a lack of appropriate information and awareness among professionals, and a lack of peer support* (R4). For older people *professional 'know best' attitudes can be a barrier, as illustrated by assumptions made by agencies about people's interest in taking up Direct Payments* (R2). Older people have expressed interest in taking up Direct Payments, as long as support was available: *a crucial element [is] … the recognition of good support systems, including access to advisors and peer support networks* (R2). Without appropriate support, older people have reported feeling *more like supplicants than purchasers* (R2) when dealing with service providers. There are similar issues for people with learning difficulties and the NHS SDO review notes that *the degree of support that users receive in recruiting and employing personal care can impact heavily on the 'success' of these schemes from the perspective of users, as well as on the conditions of employment experienced by employed workers* (R6).

Although Direct Payments give people greater flexibility and choice about who provides their individual assistance, the review noted that *homecare is provided by imperfect local markets currently characterised by lack of information for both users and workers* (R6), a situation which can impede exercise of choice for both concerned. **In some cases the limited choice has led to the establishment of user-controlled service providers (such as Centres for Independent Living for disabled people and self-advocacy groups for people with learning difficulties) and services by and for black and minority ethnic people.** Evaluation of user-led organisations for disabled people has shown that *there was overwhelming agreement that user-led organisations were far more responsive to disabled people's support needs both in terms of what was on offer and how it was delivered, with peer support a major consideration* (R4). However, the issue of regional inconsistency extends to the availability of user-controlled services for disabled people, with the majority clustered in South East England. Although user-controlled or user-led agencies may be able to provide quality services, they must nonetheless compete in a marketplace where *established non-user-led agencies enjoy a distinct advantage over user-led organisations in the current 'social care' marketplace … many health service and local authority staff have difficulty distinguishing between user and non-user-led organisations, or appear far more comfortable dealing with the latter* (R4).

### 4.4.3. Complaints

Local authorities have formal complaints procedures intended to enable individuals to exercise some control over the quality of services. The intention is to increase accountability, improve customer relations, promote quality assurance and prevent conflict or litigation. Potentially the data from the complaints feedback mechanism could be used as an indicator of service quality and possible areas for change and improvement. However, **the research suggests that such procedures may not be functioning to the advantage of the service user or the agency as complaints procedures can remain unknown or inaccessible to service users.**

The findings for children, young people and their families were clearest. The review states that *although all local authorities have complaints procedures there is evidence that a sizeable proportion of children are unaware of their existence … [research indicates] that there are long delays in dealing with complaints, that attempts to resolve complaints informally can inhibit access to the formal procedures, and that there is a continuing need for staff training and support to ensure that the procedures operate fairly and efficiently* (R1). The review recommends that *access to independent advocates can help ensure that children are better informed about their rights ... and better able to make use of complaints procedures* (R1). In addition, *parents as advocates for children fear that complaints to children's services may put children at risk of retaliation* (R6). There are similar issues for older people as *elderly people in residential care [can be] reluctant and ill-informed 'consumers', easily intimidated by fear of those they may wish to complain of* (R6).

The NHS SDO general review of literature on this topic showed that for service users wanting to change or improve services, complaints procedures may not work effectively. This can be because of the *disparity in status between complainants and the professionals they complain of, which may be exacerbated in contexts where users are 'coerced' into 'using' services (eg the families of abused children). In reality, departments may not publicise their procedures adequately, given the range of vulnerable, sensorily impaired and non-English speakers they provide services to* (R6). **People may be reluctant to use the complaints system because they are concerned about possible repercussions or fear loss of services. In general, but highlighted for people with learning difficulties and older people,** *service users may not know what local authorities are required to provide making it hard for users to know when current provision is unsatisfactory* (R6).

## 4.5. Organisational commitment and responsiveness

Despite the overall lack of research or recorded knowledge illuminating the relationship between user participation and service change and improvement, the reviews show strong indications of why change may not be occurring. Organisational responsiveness was an issue common to all the reviews. What do agencies and services do with the reported needs, recommendations and action points generated through participation exercises? Are they acted upon? Although the findings from the reviews suggest there is little evidence about whether action is taking place as a result of user involvement, general and specific barriers to change can be identified.

The NHS SDO literature review reports that **frequently cited barriers to successful user involvement include professional and organisational resistance** (R6). For mental health service users, the review *suggests that the role of organisational culture is key in both facilitating or impeding user/carer involvement in change management* (R5). Within the learning difficulties field *large gaps between policy, action (practice) and knowledge* (R3) have been reported, while with services for disabled people *the establishment of mechanisms for consultation or involvement is not always translated into meaningful changes* (R4), yet *the assumption is that being involved in negotiating decisions will be followed by meaningful cooperation in their implementation* (R4). The situation is similar for children and young people as *the evidence from the few evaluations that exist suggests that the participation of children and young people is having little impact on decisions made in relation to agency policy and practice* (R1).

Similarly, for older people *the review indicates that the main barriers for service users in affecting change in services relate to how ready social and health care agencies are to respond to the increasingly clear messages from users about the type of services that are important to them and the way they are delivered. The review raises serious questions of political, organisational and professional commitment to act on users' views* (R2). The review for older people gives further emphasis to the importance of commitment: *the issue, in terms of achieving change seems to be less one of finding effective ways of engaging older people, than that of a commitment to responding to the views so clearly expressed by older service users.* **If organisations are serious about listening to users, they also** *need to be prepared to make radical changes of approach in order to take on board what ... people are saying and address this within mainstream services* (R2). This was also found to be the case for other service users.

The findings indicate that **a fundamental political commitment to change should be driving the participation agenda. The intention to change as a result of user participation should be established prior to its implementation.** The Audit Commission emphasises this: *consultation should relate clearly to a decision that the authority plans to make, and is open to influence. It should be made clear 'what consultees can change by responding to the consultation' (and by implication what cannot be changed)* (R6). For children and young people *the point made in the literature that even though training and other events might be very good, they are unlikely to make a difference if the political will for participation is lacking* (R1). For people with learning difficulties *where there is a strong commitment and involvement is truly 'embedded' in the culture of an organisation, then a true partnership can emerge, where the involvement of people with learning difficulties leads to solid changes* (R3). The review for the participation of disabled people directs these key questions at those developing and planning services: *how committed are you? What are your main reasons for involving people?... Are you prepared to act on what they tell you? How will you deal with the change in the balance of power that meaningful involvement brings?* (R4).

Given that organisational commitment and responsiveness have been identified as general factors that could inhibit user-led service change and quality enhancement, what specific issues are involved?

## 4.6. Power relations

The principal barriers identified in the literature are the power differentials and dynamics between service users and professionals. **Power issues underlie the majority of identified difficulties with effective user-led change. The message is that any user participation initiative requires continual awareness of the context of power relations in which it is being conducted.** These power relations are historical and can pervade at both systemic and individual levels. The traditional division between service user and professional is rooted in history of 'welfare' in the UK. Historically, people who use social services were seen as passive recipients of charity and care. Decision-making power about that care traditionally lay in the hands of the providers, as did the opportunity to assert expertise. This situation has been challenged and eroded through the efforts of service users and their allies. Recent legislation has marked a theoretical movement away from paternalistic to partnership-based approaches. However, the reviews reveal that **exclusionary structures, institutional practices and attitudes can still affect the extent to which service users can influence change. It appears that power sharing can be difficult within established mainstream structures, formal consultation mechanisms and traditional ideologies.**

The NHS SDO general literature review on user involvement in change revealed various problems with systems and power: *employee respondents to a survey of local authorities suggested that 'administrative systems are designed to support institutions rather than people'.... Other difficulties, shared by other sectors, include lack of clarity about how far managers 'were really prepared to go along the consultation – participation – power sharing continuum'. Others pointed out the dangers of grafting 'token' users or carers onto existing planning and operational structures ... either the user and carer become institutionalised, or both sides continue to have very different agendas* (R6). Research concerning the involvement of people with learning difficulties indicates that *effective interaction within a consultation can only happen when there is an attempt to redress the power balance between managers/policy makers and people with learning difficulties* (R3). It is also emphasised that *professionals still exercise considerable power over disabled people's lives. Each profession assumes a language, a set of values and practices that privileges the practitioner. Hitherto, a clear division between the expert provider and lay user has reinforced their enhanced status* (R4).

**Specific problems with power sharing are further highlighted in the reviews, including notions of expertise, dominant professional perspectives and attitudes towards service user decision-making capability.** Generally, the NHS SDO report identified *professional power, assumptions about expert knowledge, professional defensiveness and lack of organisational expertise in engaging with service users* as impeding the process of change (R6). Similarly, *resistant organisation or professional cultures and embedded power differentials are seen as primary obstacles to user involvement in formal representative structures* for mental health service users (R5). For children and young people *constructive and ongoing involvement in decision making is more likely in organisations which have developed a participatory culture: one in which children are encouraged to participate in small as well as big decisions. Empowering children in this way may require adults to rethink how they share their power* (R1). The literature review for mental health service users emphasises that power is still located within the traditional arena of those who control resources: *in a 'pluralistic' or network model of public service stakeholding, users become one of many different interests. Their demands must be offset against those of other (including more powerful) stakeholders. Managers retain power at the centre of a network mediating the competing interests of professionals, users, carers, the public and political actors. A shift from top-down hierarchies to more inclusive networks or markets in the organisation of public services in these ways can produce new techniques for legitimising managerial and professional power* (R5).

The reviews show that **the relative values placed on different types of expertise and language and the professional assumptions about decision-making competence can make it difficult for users to be heard, or to make an impact on decisions:** *user/carer interests were often described as personal rather than strategic ... illustrating the mismatch between the client's experiential perspective and language, and the managerial provider perspective and language. Users of health and social care services frequently complain of the unreasonable expectation that they present their views in managerial language: failing to do so may mean those views are never considered seriously* (R6). **There remains the need for a move towards recognising the validity and respecting the worth of the unique expertise that service users have developed through experience.** Some mental health service users now favour the term 'experts by experience'. A passage from the review for people with learning difficulties exemplifies the general situation: *people with learning difficulties come to the table so that they can bring 'lived experience' of themselves and those they represent. Partnership boards need to be careful to maximise this gift, not to engulf it in professionally driven agendas* (R3). It is emphasised that *people with learning difficulties who get involved with changes can vastly improve the process because they can ground the decisions in their own lived experience* (R3).

Specific issues about the language of expertise are detailed in the review for disabled people: *a further problem for professionals is that their claim to expertise and self-regulation does not sit easily with user participation. All too often the end result is a range of initiatives in which user involvement is little more than tokenistic or seen as an exercise in user education: where agendas are dominated by professional or agency jargon, are confined to existing services or predetermined decisions in which their (user) experience is denied or minimised* (R4). Likewise, the value placed on experiential knowledge and the language for its expression has also been an issue for people who use mental health services: *the experiential knowledge of users may be valued for its authenticity but when set beside knowledges which can claim status of 'evidence' that authenticity occupies second place. In addition, the direct experience of users and the way it is expressed may sometimes be dismissed as too distressing or disturbing* (R5). The review for people with learning difficulties stresses that participation initiatives should be prepared to accommodate and value the expression of *strong feelings* (R3). Research from the voluntary sector indicates that *good quality, two-way communication between users and decision makers benefited users and promoted change in organisations. An emphasis on dialogue highlighted that the views of both parties were equally valid*[11].

**Difficulties with professional ideas of 'competency' or decision-making ability/ responsibility are indicated in the reviews for people with learning difficulties, children and young people and mental health service users.** For those involved in mental health services, *user involvement is pervaded by ambivalence. On the one hand the experience of services is seen as a direct and authentic expression of what is acceptable and what is not. On the other, being mentally ill is itself seen to disrupt the possibility of rational action* (R5). In some cases it has been assumed that people who use services can be inherently incapable of making decisions about basic things besides service change. For example *those deemed mentally ill have ... been denied full citizenship rights on the basis of lack of 'competence'* (R5). The general indications are that *in all areas of involvement, 'information giving and consultation were most common, and only very rarely are users and carers given full decision-making power'* (R6). But for people with learning difficulties, and others, **the ability to participate fully in decision making is often determined by circumstances rather than 'competence'**: *people with learning difficulties often report that they are controlled by their own service staff; their power to be influential in change is limited by: their lack of information about options and possibilities; the attitudes of staff towards self-advocacy; the entrenched interests of the service system* (R3). With regard to the role of the supporter in user participation initiatives, self-advocates have recommended that supporters need to *break from the service tradition, in which people with learning disabilities are usually engulfed, and assist people in overturning the power balance* (R3). With children and young people there can be a degree of professional anxiety about sharing power and responsibility: *adults should recognise that encouraging participation does not mean handing over responsibility for decision making to children. Children themselves are clear that while they want to be able to express their views, they do not necessarily expect to have control over final decisions* (R1). This shows the value of establishing what children and young people want and expect from participation at the outset.

**Despite some professional misgivings about user expertise and decision-making ability, it is also reported that service users who are assertive and articulate may be seen as 'unrepresentative' and therefore at risk of being ignored.** *It appears to be a particular problem that users and carers are asked to be more 'representative' than any other group of stakeholders in the change management process. Articulate users may be criticised as unrepresentative because 'ordinary' users are often not seen as articulate* (R5). **Service users who articulate the need for changes that agencies may not be willing or able to implement have sometimes been labelled as 'unrepresentative'**: *implementing changes suggested by service users that are cost neutral and make services more efficient is a relatively simple task. Implementing changes that require reallocation of resources becomes* *more difficult, especially if these conflict with nationally defined service priorities. In such instances the validity of user views or the representativeness of service users who participate may be questioned* (R6). **Concern about achieving 'representativeness' (although not necessarily diversity in terms of culture, race, sexuality or disability) is identified in most of the reviews.** With children and young people, the search for perfect representativeness in a single forum has been identified as an inhibiting factor, and it is suggested that *developing a range of methods to reach different groups of people can be preferable to trying to achieve perfect 'representativeness' in one setting* (R1). Disabled people have expressed concerns that *user representation is too closely regulated by managers* (R4).

**An enhanced social and political understanding of the user movement among professionals may improve understanding of service user representation issues.** For example, for people with learning difficulties, *if we consider self-advocacy to be a social movement, similar to the social movements of black people or women, then it is perfectly possible for the active members to represent others and fight on their behalf* (R3). It is also noted that *the active involvement of older people in enabling others to have a say is another trend and represents a move away from the tendency reporting in earlier reviews of speaking 'for' older people* (R2). **Many service user controlled organisations and advocacy schemes have innovative approaches to participation, and have a distinctive role in empowering users to collectively take action. Issues of inclusion and representation should be addressed with service users. It appears that agencies have a responsibility, in collaboration with users, to undertake checks (eg through user-led surveys) about how strategies resulting from user involvement match the expectations and wishes of all service users.**

## 4.7. Partnership or consultancy?

There is some indication in the review findings that **user participation initiatives can become consultation exercises to approve of service planning and policy proposals, rather than enabling service users to be key players or partners in their formulation.** For example, research examining attitudes towards the participation of older people found that *professionals … expressed disappointment with the 'negativity of expressed opinions', while 'officials seemed more comfortable with the idea of soliciting views on matters of immediate concern to them than with responding to the user panels as a pressure group (a term which they introduced…'* (R6). The reviews show that many organisations have an understanding of participation that still positions service users as external consultants rather than partners in the development process. *In the social care field, local authorities and agencies tend to use one-off consultation processes generally in order to comply with the requirement to consult users as part of an initiative directed by central government…. Less common is the sort of activity designed to enable children and young people to have an ongoing involvement in the work of the agency* (R1). Mental health service users report that *models of change management generally position service users as external stakeholders* (R5), suggesting that they often remain outside the central sphere of influence and decision making. However, **the research suggests that embedded participation based on a partnership approach could be most effective at achieving lasting change.** For example, *involving people with learning difficulties as partners in change must be a process that is 'embedded in the culture' of an organisation. There have to be structures for continuing to work together and to hear the voice of people who use services* (R3). Generally, the reviews reveal *there is a danger that government demands for agencies to demonstrate user involvement may mean that user activities become a formal procedure to be ticked* *off rather than an embedded and powerful organisational practice* (R5).

The work on disabled people and mental health service users highlights an emerging trend termed 'the technology of legitimation', in which managers seek user approval for their decisions: **some critics argue that user involvement is too easily exploited as a 'technology of legitimation'. Thus, it sustains management and government authority by giving the appearance of democratising public services without allowing policy shifts in 'undesirable' directions.** *Indeed, managers and professionals are both prone to 'play the user card' in trying to win a policy dispute* (R4). *Strategies of user involvement can work to reinforce the power of professionals and managers. This is especially the case where the 'user card' is played strategically so as to bolster certain professional interests against other organisational interests* (R5). Indications of such legitimating activity have also been found for children and young people: *forums, the method used most commonly by local authorities, are least popular with young people and not something they suggest. Significant problems have been identified with this type of activity: often they lack a sense of purpose, are not well integrated with local decision making structures, are not accountable to other young people in the area, and are seen as a token group of young people used to legitimise adult decisions* (R1).

Some discussion has centred on the role of participation 'champions' or leaders in promoting cultural change and organisational commitment. While it has been asserted that *user involvement requires 'champions' throughout the organisation for it to flourish* (R4), **the role of professional allies remains under-explored**: *it is notable that a mainly professionally authored literature appears to ignore the important role of professional user involvement 'champions'* (R5). There are concerns that agencies may rely solely on the commitment of one individual rather than embedding participation in organisational practice, and that individual managers may only be interested in the role for career advancement. *On the other hand, some user authors take a more positive approach to those professionals whom they perceive to have helped sustain the momentum of a user group* (R5). One study indicated that, within the voluntary sector *people in leadership roles, who were influential within existing power structures and who operated a facilitative leadership style, opened up opportunities for users to have influence themselves*[12]. It is also possible that professional allies could themselves identify as service users, thus adding another dimension to the debate.

Research suggests that **embedded, continuous but varied participation approaches that engage service users in decision making have most potential for influencing change. The majority of service users wish to represent themselves directly, collectively or through a peer advocate in decision-making forums.** The less favoured approach is having input mediated through external consultation exercises and questionnaires that could be vulnerable to different professional interpretations. **Service users should be understood as active partners, albeit in an often unequal partnership.** It is argued that **there is no single solution or technique for enabling service users to participate in service and policy planning and development,** and *involvement [should move away] from purely consultation-based methods towards a wider range of different forms of participation* (R2).

Finally, **agencies are recommended to re-examine their notion of service users who are thought to be 'hard to reach'.** Some service users *may lack structures of representation; may find it difficult to meet with [other] service users and managers; or may be hampered by attitudinal and legislative deficiencies that fail to promote their rights to involvement* (R6). Paradoxically, it is indicated that for some service users (eg, older people with dementia), those who remain excluded from participation processes may be those who make higher use of services. For older people with dementia, this has prompted the recommendation for consultation to become *an integral part of ongoing individual care* (R2).

## 4.8. Conflict and expectations

*Biehal*[13] *discusses consultation with users as an aid to greater managerial efficiency, but warns that 'this will not necessarily be accompanied by any real increase in the power of service users to determine the range and quality of the services available to them'. Discrepancy between what managers want of user involvement and what users want may be a major source of dissatisfaction for service users (since the managers' definitions tend to prevail)* (R6). Some reviews note that **dissatisfaction and even conflict may be an inevitable part of the user participation process.** Self-advocates assert that for people with learning difficulties speaking up is *not just about having polite interactions around the table* (R3) and *the most clear-cut examples of self-advocacy led initiatives are local and reactive: they are protests made against decisions by others* (R3). Mental health service users' experience of the participation process has shown that *it is a mistake to assert that conflicts should or can be resolved before the process of change is begun. Power differentials between users and professionals and differences in perceptions of satisfactory outcomes mean that conflict is to be expected.... The management and resolution of conflict is an on-going function of change management* (R5).

At the front-line level *there can be tension between workers and users/carers. Managers and other staff may see user involvement as both of value and a threat. One way of understanding this is as a conflict between staff and managers' desire to implement a rather limited consumerist agenda and the hunger of many users to reclaim their spoiled identity and reassert themselves as citizens.*

*User involvement in change management will work best when front-line staff and other stakeholders are also meaningfully engaged in organisational processes. However, conflicts will inevitably arise between the various actors* (R5). Again, people with learning difficulties have found that the engagement of front-line staff in user participation is needed, but there can be a disparity between policy makers, management and front-line staff: *one of the main points ... was about the importance of staff in services, particularly in day services. [Self-advocates] commented 'people at the top listen, but not those at the bottom'* (R3). The research suggests that **front-line practitioners who have most contact with service users could be usefully engaged in user participation strategies and benefit from user-led training focusing on the practice and principles of user participation**. This could go some way to preventing uncertainty about user participation *where front-line workers re-interpret organisational guidelines and policies in their day-to-day practice* (R4) and addressing the possible *deficit in the skills and commitment of front-line workers to listen to and act on users' views* (R2). The motivation and commitment of front-line practitioners can also be compromised by organisational structures and audit cultures. **Organisations and their managers should support front-line practitioners to focus on user concerns, as they may be inhibited from doing so by unhelpful processes or timetables.** Research has shown that user-centred activity within the voluntary sector was promoted where leaders: *created space for users and staff to debate user involvement and to develop and try out ideas [and] encouraged and supported users and staff*[14].

**Limited financial and other resources along with conflicting priorities emerge from the reviews as restraints on the degree to which service users may be able to influence changes in services. There may be restrictions on the ability of an organisation to respond positively, including its service remit.** User research has shown that the need for a holistic approach to support: *other services were very important to people beyond ideas of social care, in particular housing and information*[15]. The reviews recommend that **agencies should be clear from the outset about what can and cannot be done as a result of participation and the true extent of user influence in the given circumstances**: *organisations need to be very clear about the scope for service users to influence services, and also about the constraints. Lack of honest information can create confusion and disillusionment as well as preventing meaningful engagement and change (R2)*. Similarly, **service users should be empowered to voice their limits and expectations.** These approaches could go some way to preventing unnecessary conflict during the process.

*Research describing the integration of user and carer involvement highlights the need to resolve 'tensions between approaches designed to encourage user participation on the one hand, and meeting the requirements of planning systems on the other'…. Mismatches in timing, participation and meeting methods and expectations, financial constraints and coordination difficulties all arose, with planning groups unable to meet tight timetables effectively marginalised despite the effort expended by participants. Control and power remains with practitioner/managers, whose guiding principles may be financial (R6). Professionals may sometimes comment on unreasonable expectations of users who choose not to consider financial restraints and imperatives, while it may be that users are not permitted to consider them (R6).* For disabled people *user involvement has increased over recent years. While this has been welcomed by disabled people and their organisations, it has also exposed the limitations of the rhetoric of empowerment within a 'social care' environment that is subject to tight budgetary controls (R4).* The findings from the review for older people points towards organisational capacity to change: *when service users are asked for their views, it produces a substantial agenda for change, which has to compete with the organisation's more immediate pressures or other perceived priorities (R2).* Managers have *relative operational autonomy but only within strict budgetary controls and performance targets. In such an organisational environment there is far less opportunity for partnership with disabled people … user-led agendas [risk being] overtaken by a contrary set of political and economic constraints (R4).* It has also been argued that financial constraints on social care services have contributed to the development of some services that are crisis-led, rather than being able to offer the preventative support and assistance that some service users say they need. On a wider level, *central and local policy direction may work against what users want (R2).*

**Development of mutual understanding, effective communication and conflict resolution takes time but review findings show that the pace of work itself can be exclusionary and could potentially affect the quality of engagement with service users.** *People who have been excluded need to be able to trust the people they are working with, to know that other people will take them seriously and will do what they say they are going to do*[16]. Working to timetables determined without input from service users may result in the exclusion of some people or limit their effective participation because *pace and volume of work has to be appropriate (R3)*. Self-advocates feel *strongly that the process of change needs to slow down, and to be more thorough, so that involvement does not become tokenistic (R3)*, while research for older people points to the importance of allowing time and space for effective participation, particularly for more marginalised older people such as those who are frail and housebound or have dementia. Disabled people's evaluation of participation processes identified the fact that there was *too little time for meaningful discussion (R4).* Time as a barrier was also identified in the review for children and young people which stresses that *time is needed to set up projects properly, and to listen and hear what young people are really* *saying can be underestimated. Deadlines for completing tasks can also be drawn too tightly to be realistic* (R1). The resourcing and core funding of user participation and user groups was explored by several reviews. **The findings point to the importance of supporting user groups to maintain their independence and critical function**: *some measure of independent and critical thinking is necessary to make changes happen at a fundamental level, so that involvement does not simply mean collusion* (R3). Elsewhere it is noted that *funding user-controlled organisations as a means of developing user involvement is identified as good practice*[17]. The provision of specific budgets for user participation has also been identified as a potential change enabler, with the allocation of money also demonstrating *a tangible commitment beyond its practical use*[18]. Again, resourcing appears ultimately to be a power sharing issue.

## 4.9. Diversity and marginalisation

The reviews showed that attention to the **diversity of service users in terms of race, culture, sexuality and, in some cases, disability was lacking in mainstream services and participation initiatives**. This relates to both diversity within user groups and the relative lack of knowledge about user participation for marginalised people. **Service users who are marginalised from mainstream services can also be found to be under- or unrepresented in the participation intended to develop those services**. The majority of research identified in the reviews concerned issues for black and minority ethnic people.

It has already been established that at the level of individual service provision, the needs of black and minority ethnic people and those who identify as lesbian or gay are not being adequately addressed. This has, in some cases, resulted in the development of particular user-led service providers aiming to meet those needs: *users who feel marginalised or inadequately provided for by mainstream or statutory services may move towards establishing voluntary sector services, aiming to provide mutual support and advocacy against discriminatory practices and institutions* (R6). Consistent with this, the review of Social Services Inspectorate reports revealed that much of the service provision for black and minority ethnic older people is in the voluntary sector. For the mental health service user movement there are *two strands to empowerment for Black and Asian users: 'reactive' measures that respond to existing problems in service provision (this includes advocacy and legal representation and training for black users); and 'innovative' measures that focus on forms of self-organisation as well as campaigning for reforms within the mental health system* (R5). This approach is reflected in the work of black and minority ethnic and lesbian and gay disabled people, who are also working on the margins of a predominantly white, middle-class, culturally heterosexual user movement.

**The challenge to mainstream services is to creatively engage marginalised peoples, the concerns of whom often extend beyond service provision to creating positive social and political identities in the face of discrimination**: *Black and minority ethnic groups may have difficulty in subordinating their objectives to the narrow [services] agenda, and may be unwilling to act as collaborators ... it [has been] argued that for some people previous attempts to influence health and social care services have proved so unsatisfactory that separation is less demoralising* (R6). Some participation projects seeking to gain knowledge of minority ethnic community priorities can over-rely on community spokespeople and 'leaders' who may not always be able to represent the spectrum of voices within that community (this is an issue particularly highlighted for women). There are fewer efforts to *investigate service needs than to engage with 'the community' or the 'power brokers' in the community, in more superficial ways* (R6). Black and minority ethnic elders have reported feeling *over-*

*researched; they wanted to see some effective action and to become involved in decisions that affected them* (R2). In addition, *service users may also be stereotyped according to the expectations of service providers* (R6), such as the myth of extended families providing care for older and disabled relatives.

As regards the participation of people with learning difficulties *one of the big challenges is to hear the voices of all those who are supposedly represented by [the] process, including those from black and minority ethnic communities and people with high support needs. The present review revealed very few examples of initiatives specifically aiming to engage them in planning or research* (R3). For older people, *while there are pockets of good practice, the overall impression is that basic communication with minority ethnic groups is still at a rudimentary stage* (R2); *our analysis endorses the points made by other research reviews that there is a need for better understanding of issues relating to exploring and supporting the involvement of: older gay and lesbian people; people living with long-term conditions and disabilities; black and minority ethnic older people; people in rural areas* (R2). The situation is very similar for children and young people as well as disabled people and mental health service users: *structural and cultural barriers contribute to an under-representation of some groups among disabled users. These include people from minority ethnic groups, lesbians and gays and younger disabled people* (R4). *There is evidence that alternative methods, as opposed to formal processes, of consulting children are rarely used, indicating possibly a lack of sufficient staff with the skills to communicate with children, particularly young children and disabled children* (R1). The *lack of information [to inform decision making] in minority ethnic languages* (R1) for children and young people is also highlighted for older people and other groups.

The reviews show that marginalisation from both appropriate services and participation processes does not only occur because of race, culture and sexuality. **Living in rural or certain geographical areas can have a bearing on exclusion from structures for participation. The very young and the very old, particularly those with dementia, the homeless and travellers, people in institutional or residential care, people with addiction problems and those with severe disabilities and high support needs (including learning difficulties) or needs that cut across traditional service categories (ie young black disabled people), seldom have the opportunity to be heard or to influence service change. It is also recommended that poverty should be considered as an important overarching issue.** Research shows that people living in poverty *often do not know they have a right to a say – no one has ever asked them their opinion. And when they do know, they are often denied the opportunity to exercise it because of a lack of resources, support, education, self-confidence or the respect of others*[19].

A key message from the review for children and young people could also apply to other people who are often excluded from the participation process: *little is known about why young people choose not to be involved, or why they get excluded … of relevance there is the definition of use of the term 'hard to reach'. There is a danger in seeing this as something to do with the children and young people themselves rather than a reflection of an agency's ability to communicate with a wide range of children and families* (R1). Increased awareness is recommended: *in addition to promoting organisational cultures that are conducive to user involvement in general, arguments also arise in this field about the need for cultural sensitivity on the part of professionals and organisations in relation to different user needs* (R5), as is the need for adequate resourcing: *the expansion of … self-advocacy groups, and the 'mainstreaming' of minority issues in wider … services, will be constrained by lack of resources unless a commitment to minority ethnic needs can be built into the contract culture in health and social services* (R5). Finally, **for marginalised people and for user participation generally it seems that** *the fundamental challenge is to leave behind the apparent security offered by categorical approaches, in favour of more temporary and incomplete processes of policy and services development that will mark a significant departure from traditional forms of bureaucratic management* (R6).

# The Wiltshire and Swindon User Network: an example in practice

The Wiltshire and Swindon User Network (WSUN) was formed in 1991 in response to directives in the 1990 NHS and Community Care Act which identified service users as key stakeholders in social care. The social model of disability was important to the conception of a network of people which cut across traditional service group categories: *from the start we sought to maintain the balance between specialist users' groups needing to meet together within the Network, while celebrating the commonality of our disempowerment and the strength and confidence we gained from being one Network*[20]. In 1993 the Network had 300 local contacts and received core funding from Wiltshire Social Services community care infrastructure budget. A service agreement was drawn up: *we sought to protect our independence by ensuring that the service agreement was legally binding so that funding could not be withdrawn as a 'knee jerk' reaction to criticism. We also wrote our own service specification; but in reality, our belief that such funding would not affect our right to speak out, grew more from the fragile trust that has already been developed between users and the [Social Services] Department and joint recognition of the on-going tension and power imbalances between users and professionals*[21]. The Network continues to have a *local, user-led, bottom-up approach to community care planning ... embedded in the system*[22].

WSUN has a proactive, personal outreach approach and provides peer support and space for service users to share experiences and gain confidence. Regular meetings are held to discuss subjects of concern and to identify gaps for planning. WSUN then arranges direct user participation in service planning, provision and evaluation and *active Network members are ... able to empower users not yet heard*[23]. They stress the importance of getting the right infrastructure for service users to develop user participation on their own terms and the value of social services allies. The following core principles have been identified which inform the development of user-controlled organisations seeking to promote service change:

- user-led community development work;
- social model of disability;
- valuing user expertise and energy;
- building on existing user initiatives;
- working with allies;
- change of expertise from knowing best to enabling;
- beginning a journey of exploration;
- riddling the system;
- bite-sized chunks;
- bottom-up change[24].

WSUN has been employed in these policy and service provision developments:

- leading in policy development – influencing commissioning and purchasing decisions;
- power sharing in resource management – designing and controlling the Wiltshire Independent Living Fund;
- developing user controlled-services – information and support services for those using independent living funds (including specialist advice for people from minority ethnic backgrounds) and advocacy work;
- user input into care management procedures – redesigning referral,

assessment and review processes, retraining staff;
- staff and student training – group approach to bring a variety of perspectives, training social workers and educating social work students;
- evaluation – user-controlled Best Value review of Direct Payments[25].

Finally, commenting on the effectiveness of user participation, WSUN's former director has written: *the energy and expertise of service users supported by our own organisation, combined with the commitment of senior welfare professionals to use their personal power to enable us to gain a position of power and influence, has given us a vision of user-controlled services characterised by users' choice and control and the recognition of users as major stakeholders. The future will show whether users' energy and expertise, together with allies' commitment, is strong enough to resist the constraints of rationing, lack of resources and society's expectations of welfare agencies as agents of social control, to bring about long-term changes in inequalities in service provision*[26].

# Conclusion: messages for policy and practice

This concluding section briefly outlines some of the significant messages from the overview for practitioners, managers and policy makers.

Factors to consider when planning and implementing service user participation for service enhancement and change include the following:

1. Be clear about the aims and scope of participation before starting the process.

2. Identify and engage any existing local or regional user initiatives.

3. Clearly communicate the aims and scope to potential participants from the outset in appropriate, accessible ways.

4. Before participation begins ensure there is political will and organisational commitment to change and sufficient resources to actively address service user priorities.

5. Ensure that user participation is responsive to the perspectives, priorities, needs and aims of local service users. These may not match traditional service categories or managerial service priorities.

6. Be aware of the power relations between service user and professional throughout the process.

7. Consider ways to prevent or creatively manage any conflict together with the participants and remain aware of the need to share information and decision-making power.

8. Value the knowledge and expertise of people who use services and ensure that this can be communicated in ways that they are comfortable with.

9. Work towards creating diverse, flexible, continuous participation strategies that are integral to the decision-making structures of an organisation. These should be appropriate to and planned with service users so be prepared to rethink those structures to accommodate new ways of working and communicating.

10. Make sure that adequate time and resources are available to support effective, inclusive participation.

11. Plan a framework to monitor and evaluate the impact of participation with the involved service users, as well as the experience of the process itself.

12. During process plan with participants how feedback will communicated to them and how to respond further if required.

13. Address any issues of representation with service users.

14. Think creatively and consult on different ways to involve people who may otherwise be marginalised from the process.

15. Ensure that all staff involved (including front-line workers) understand the principles and practice of service user participation and are empowered by organisational structures, processes and management strategies to make it a success.

*Source:* compiled with reference to R6.

## 6.1. Messages from the research for policy makers

This overview suggests that efforts to involve people in the planning and development of the services they use are taking place across the UK. What remains unclear is the impact of that participation. At local and regional levels policy makers would be advised to integrate change mapping and feedback into the whole participation process. Monitoring and evaluation techniques should be developed with service users. At national level a programme of research addressing the outcomes, at different levels, of different approaches to user involvement could be instigated and developed in partnership with service users. Seen within a larger framework defined by stages, it seems that first stage of establishing the principle of service user participation and developing participation processes has been reached. The research in this overview points to a transition from this first, adaptive stage to a second stage of transformational change[27]. This means looking at how organisations can transform (both culturally, structurally and in terms of policy and practice development) in response to service user participation, now the principle has been established.

Professionals now need to interact with service users as partners in strategic planning arenas as well as at front-line service delivery level. As a result the stereotyped ideas about service users, dominant professional perspectives on expertise and the language for its expression, conflicting priorities and power dynamics are among the factors that may be impeding progress. The research shows the importance of allowing sufficient time and support for constructive dialogue and trust building to improve partnership working. *In order to change practices, professionals … need to have contact with users and carers outside the details of the individual care packages*[28]. It appears that involving front-line staff in participation strategies and providing user-led awareness training could help improve user/professional relations at both strategic and service delivery level. Supported, open and respectful communication is key.

Challenges to traditional professional modes of thinking and operating are emerging as a result of participation. The reviews indicate that organisational culture and structure also needs to respond and change in order to accommodate new partnerships and new ways of working with people who have often been oppressed and marginalised. There are things to learn about innovative and collective approaches to participation and change from user-controlled organisations such as centres for independent/inclusive living and self-advocacy schemes. Organisations require policies and procedures (formulated with service users) that engender positive political commitment and minimise resistance to user-led change. User-led research could usefully reveal more about the role of professional allies in promoting change.

The issue of power sharing needs to be openly discussed at every level so that users and professionals have the opportunity to share experiences, explore the meaning of partnership and independence and develop new structures and approaches to service, and indeed organisational development. The desire of service users for holistic approaches to support and assistance seems to have influenced their approaches to participation. Many people want to improve and have greater control over the disparate elements of support and service in their lives and require participation strategies that can reflect this. The political and philosophical methods of the service user movement seem to be exposing the limitations of traditional, fragmented service categories for organising participation designed to promote strategic change. Participation provides a unique opportunity for organisations to develop and transform through critical enquiry with service users using the social model of disability, ideas about control, oppression, rights, poverty and citizenship.

# Additional references

1. Audit Commission (1999) *Listen up! Effective community consultation*, London: Audit Commission.

2. UPIAS (Union of the Physically Impaired Against Segregation) (1975) *Fundamental principles of disability*, London: UPIAS.

3. ATD Fourth World (2002) *Annual Review 2002*, London: ATD Fourth World, p 9.

4. Beresford, P., Croft, S., Evans, C. and Harding, T. (1997) 'Quality in personal social services: the developing role of user involvement in the UK', in A. Ever, R. Haverinen, K. Leichsenring and G. Wistow (eds) *Developing quality in personal social services: Concepts, cases and comments*, European Centre, Vienna/Aldershot: Ashgate, pp 63-80 [p 65].

5. Ibid, p 63.

6. Robson, P., Begum, N. and Lock, M. (2003) Joseph Rowntree Foundation Findings: *Increasing user involvement in voluntary organisations*, York: Joseph Rowntree Foundation, p 3.

7. Audit Commission (1999) op cit.

8. Audit Commission/Social Services Inspectorate (2002) *Tracking the changes: The Joint Review Team Sixth Annual Report 2001/2*, London: Audit Commission.

9. Evans, R. and Banton, M. (2001) *Learning from experience: Involving black disabled people in shaping services*, Warwickshire: Council of Disabled People.

10. Evans, C. (1999) 'Gaining our voice: the developing pattern of good practice', *Managing Community Care*, vol 7, no 2, pp 7-13.

11. Robson, P., Begum, N. and Lock, M. (2003) op cit, p 2.

12. Ibid, p 1.

13. Biehal, N. (1993) 'Changing practice: participation, rights and community care', *British Journal of Social Work*, vol 23, pp 443-58.

14. Robson, P., Begum, N. and Lock, M. (2003) op cit, p 2.

15. Shaping Our Lives National User Network (2003) *Shaping our lives – What people think of the social care services they use*, York: Joseph Rowntree Foundation, p 1.

16. ATD Fourth World (2000) *Participation works: Involving people in poverty in policy making*, London: ATD Fourth World, p 29.

17. Evans, C. (1996) 'Service users acting as agents of change', in P. Bywaters and E. McLeod (eds) *Working for equality in health*, London: Routledge, pp 81-93 [p 83].

18. Robson, P., Begum, N. and Lock, M. (2003) op cit, p 3.

19. ATD Fourth World (2000) op cit, p 32.

20. Evans, C. (1996) op cit, p 82.

[21] Ibid, p 83.

[22] Evans, C. (1999) op cit, p 7.

[23] Evans, C. (1996) op cit, p 85.

[24] Evans, C. (1999) op cit, p 8.

[25] Evans, C. and Carmichael, A. (2002) *Users' Best Value: A guide to user involvement good practice in Best Value reviews*, York: Joseph Rowntree Foundation.

[26] Evans, C. (1996) op cit, p 92.

[27] Argyris, C. and Schön, D. (1978) *Organisational learning: A theory of action perspective*, Reading, MA: Addison-Wesley.

[28] Olsen, R., Parker, G. and Drewett, A. (1997) 'Carers and the missing link: changing professional attitudes', *Health and Social Care in the Community*, vol 5, no 2, pp 116-23 [p 117].

# Appendix

More information about the individual reviews used in this report can be obtained from the authors:

*Children and young people*
Dr Ruth Sinclair
National Children's Bureau
8 Wakley Street
London EC1V 7QE
research@ncb.org.uk

*Older people*
Karin Janzon
Care Equation Ltd
43 Hove Park Villas
Hove BN3 6HH
kjanzon@care-equation.org.uk

*People with learning difficulties*
Dr Val Williams
Norah Fry Research Centre
University of Bristol
3 Priory Road
Bristol BS8 1TX
val.williams@bristol.ac.uk

*Disabled people*
Professor Colin Barnes
Centre for Disability Studies
Department of Sociology and Social Policy
University of Leeds
Leeds LS2 9JT
disability-studies@leeds.ac.uk

*Mental health service users*
Dr Diana Rose
Service User Research Enterprise
Institute of Psychiatry
De Crespigny Park
London SE5 8AF
enquiries@iop.kcl.ac.uk

*General literature review on user involvement*
Dr Mike Crawford
Senior Lecturer in Psychiatry
Department of Psychological Medicine
Faculty of Medicine
Imperial College London
Paterson Centre
20, South Wharf Road
London W2 1PD